ABRÉVIATIONS ET SIGNES

W	=	Tout l'archet
H	=	Moitié de l'archet
L H	=	Moitié inférieure
U H	=	Moitié supérieure
⅓ B	=	Un tiers de l'archet
N	=	Talon de l'archet
M	=	Milieu de l'archet
P	=	Pointe de l'archet
M*	=	Travailler de trois façons: (1) du milieu de l'archet (2) de la pointe de l'archet (3) du talon de l'archet
⊓	=	Tirez
V	=	Poussez
—	=	Soutenu. Tiré large, avec peu d'interruption entre les notes, particulièrement entre deux et plusieurs notes sur un archet.
•	=	Staccato. Travailler séparément avec beaucoup et peu d'archet et, jouer court; laisser l'archet sur la corde lorsqu'il y a 2 ou plusieurs notes à l'archet.
Ma	=	Martelé. Coups d'archet detachés accentués, en laissant l'archet sur la corde.
Sa	=	Sautillé. Archet jeté ou sautillé avec deux ou plusieurs notes à l'archet.
⋏	=	Spiccato Très peu d'archet, en levant l'archet de la corde après chaque note.
)	=	Lever l'archet de la corde.
Legato.		Liaison souple de note à note avec pression régulière de l'archet ou en pressions variées.
*	=	A défaut de ce signe au début d'un exercice, commencer par le tiré au talon.

ABREVIATIONS AND EXPLANATIONS

W	=	Whole length of bow
H	=	Half length of bow
L H	=	Lower half of bow
U H	=	Upper half of bow
⅓ B	=	Third of bow
N	=	Nut-end (Heel of bow)
M	=	Middle of bow
P	=	Point of bow
M*	=	Practise in three ways: (1) in middle of bow (2) at the point (3) at the heel
⊓	=	Down bow
V	=	Up bow
—	=	Well sustained - may also be interpreted as broad and sustained with slight detachment between notes, especially with two or more notes in same bow.
•	=	Staccato i.e., Articulating each note separately and short, whether short or long bows, or articulating two or more notes in same bow with bow on string.
Ma	=	Martelé i.e., detached accentuated separate bows with bow on string.
Sa	=	Sautillé i.e., springing or bounding bow with two or more notes in same bow.
⋏	=	Spiccato i.e. extremely short bow with bow off the string after each note.
)	=	Bow to be raised from the string.
Legato,		i.e. smoothly or well-bound from one note to another— with even pressure of bow whether played forte or piano or with various shades of expression.
*	=	If there is no sign at the beginning of an exercise, begin the first note at the heel with a down bow.

ABKÜRZUNGEN UND ZEICHEN

W	=	Ganzer Bogen
H	=	Halber Bogen
L H	=	Untere Hälfte des Bogens
U H	=	Obere Hälfte des Bogens
⅓ B	=	Ein Drittel des Bogens
N	=	Am Frosch des Bogens
M	=	Mitte des Bogens
P	=	Spitze des Bogens
M*	=	Übe in drei Arten: (1) mit der Mitte des Bogens (2) mit der Spitze des Bogens (3) am Frosch des Bogens
⊓	=	Abstrich
V	=	Aufstrich
—	=	Gehalten. Wird breit gezogen, mit geringen Trennungen zwischen den Noten gespielt, besonders bei zwei und mehr Noten auf einem Bogen.
•	=	Staccato. Sowohl mit viel als wenig Bogen getrennt und kurz zu spielen; bei zwei und mehr Noten auf einem Bogen bleibt der Bogen auf der Saite.
Ma	=	Martelé. Getrennte, akzentuierte Bogenstriche, wobei der Bogen auf der Saite bleibt.
Sa	=	Sautillé. Springender oder geworfener Strich mit zwei oder mehr Noten auf einem Bogen.
⋏	=	Spiccato. Sehr kurze Striche, wobei der Bogen nach jeder Note von der Saite gehoben wird.
)	=	Bogen von der Saite heben.
Legato.		Geschmeidige Bindung von Note zu Note mit gleichmässigem Bogendruck oder in verschiedenen Stärkegraden.
*	=	Wenn dieses Zeichen nicht am Anfang einer Übung steht, beginnt sie immer am Frosch im Abstrich.

B.& Co.Ltd. 21692

PARTIE III (Cahier 5) EXERCICES POUR FORTIFIER LE POIGNET	THIRD PART (Section V) EXERCISES FOR DEVELOPING THE POWER OF THE WRIST	3. TEIL (Abschnitt V) ÜBUNGEN ZUR ENTWICKLUNG DER KRAFT DES HANDGELENKES

37

Exercice No.37 (à jouer selon les 1040 exemples de coups d'archet.) Dans ce premier exercice (a) efforcez-vous de jouer sur les trois cordes à la fois et d'y maintenir l'archet. Lorsque vous y serez parvenu, tâchez de compter les deux temps de chaque mesure un peu plus lentement que ne l'indique le métronome $\boldsymbol{J}$ = 84.	Exercise No.37 to be played throughout in 1040 different examples of bowing. In this first exercise (a) try to play and sustain all three strings simultaneously. When you have accomplished this endeavour to count the two beats to the bar even slower than metronome mark $\boldsymbol{J}$ = 84.	Übung Nr. 37 ist in 1040 verschiedenen Stricharten zu spielen. In dieser ersten Übung (a) versuche alle drei Saiten gleichzeitig zum Erklingen zu bringen. Wenn dies erreicht ist, versuche die zwei Taktschläge noch langsamer zu zählen, als das Metronom $\boldsymbol{J}$ = 84 angibt.

Deux fois	*Duple time*	*Allabreve*

1040 exemples de coups d'archet pour l'exercice ci-dessus.	*1040 examples of bowing for above exercise No.37.*	*1040 Beispiele verschiedener Stricharten für obige Übung Nr. 37.*

B.& Co. Ltd. 21692 c

Exercices **24** à **29** à jouer d'abord avec la moitié inférieure de l'archet et ensuite avec la moitié supérieure.

Exercise **24** to **29** first with the lower half and then with the upper half of bow.

Übung Nr. **24** bis **29** ist erst mit der unteren Hälfte, dann mit der oberen Hälfte des Bogens zu spielen.

4

Staccato

Un tiers d'archet. | Third of bow. | Ein Drittel des Bogens.

B.& Co.Ltd.21692c

Coups d'archet divers. | Various bowing. | Verschiedene Stricharten.

6

B. & Co. Ltd. 21692c

Mêmes coups d'archet 384-397
Same bowings 384-397
Dieselben Stricharten 384-397

Employez très peu d'archet. | Use very little bow. | Sehr wenig Bogen.

(Metr. ♩=120, ♩=144, ♩=176)

Tous les exemples de demi-mesure doivent être répétés deux fois.

All half bar examples must be repeated twice.

Alle halbtaktigen Beispiele sind zweimal zu wiederholen.

Mêmes coups d'archet 497-510
Same bowings 497-510
Dieselben Stricharten 497-510

10

B. & Co. Ltd. 21692 c

12

B. & Co. Ltd. 21692c

16

B.& Co. Ltd. 21692c

18

Sautillé (coups l'archet rebondissants). | Ricochet (bouncing bow). | Saltato (mit springendem Bogen).

B.& Co.Ltd.21692ᶜ

Trois cordes simultanément. | Three strings simultaneously. | Drei Saiten gleichzeitig.

PARTIE III (Cahier 6)   THIRD PART (Section VI)   3. TEIL (Abschnitt VI)

38

L'exercice No. 38 doit être joué, chaque fois en son entier, selon les **726** différents exemples de coups d'archet.

Exercise No. 38 to be practised throughout in the **726** examples of different bowings.

Übung Nr. 38 ist in **726** verschiedenen Stricharten zu spielen.

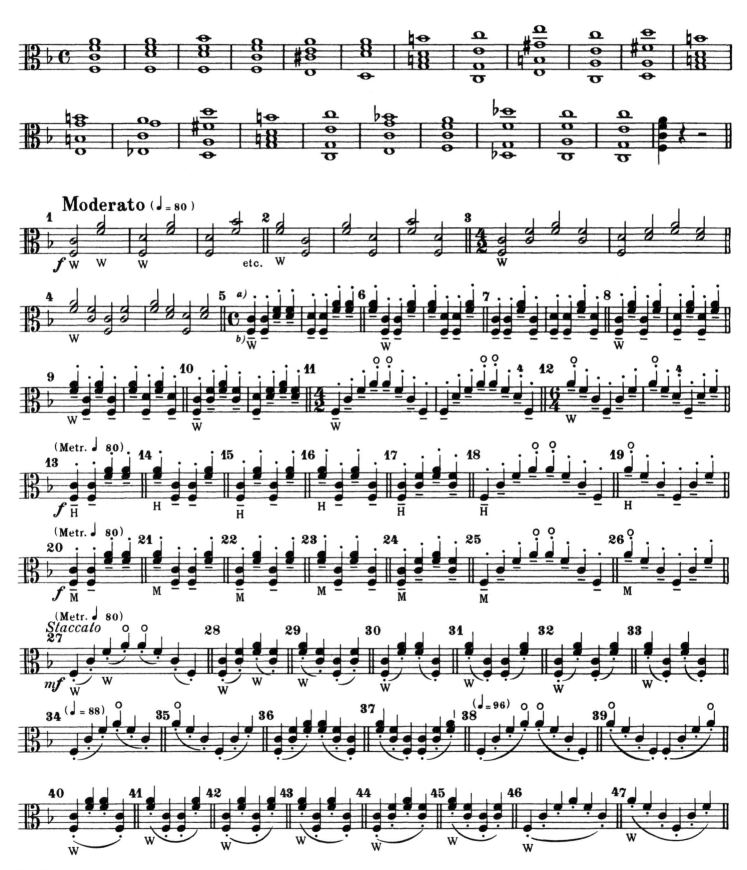

26

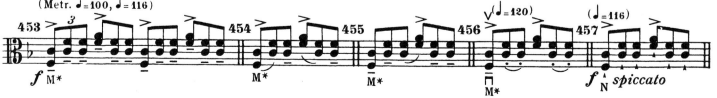

B.& Co.Ltd.21692c

Exercez le poignet. | Use your wrist. | Mit dem Handgelenk.

Legato